Are you a Cow Lover?!

By

Chakrapani Srinivasa

Are You a Cow Lover?
By
Chakrapani Srinivasa

Dedicated to our dear parents

About the Author

Chakrapani Srinivasa (Padmaja), Freelance journalist from India possesses Bachelor degree in Engineering (B.E) and Post graduate in Business Management (MBA) with Distinction. He has worked as Associate Editor of 'Naradar' fortnightly journal in Chennai, India. He is the Senior Editor of the journal "The Divineness".

Contributed articles, short stories and travelogues in leading journals like Ananda Vikatan, Kumudam, Savi, Kalki, Dinamani Kadhir, Dinamani daily, Idhayam Pesukirathu, Naradar etc

He has written articles and e books through Smashwords Inc, Kindle Direct Publishing, Atlanta publications, Cooperjal publications (UK), lulu.com, ezinearticles.com, shvoong.com, iproclaim.com (USA) and TCC news (Germany).

He is the Consulting Editor: Contemporary Who's Who-Research Board of Advisors of ABI.

Foreword

My utmost reverence to the Senior Pontiff of Pejavara Adhokshaja matha Pujyashree Sri Vishvesha theertha Swamiji and The Junior Pontiff Of Sri Pejavara Adhokshaja Matha, Sri Vishwaprasanna Theertha Swamiji, who graciously supported me in all respects to prepare this book on cow's greatness. The speeches by Sri Vishwaprasanna Theertha Swamiji in the CD on Srimad Bhagavatham (Proshtapadi) were guiding stars for this humble attempt. Several points from internet and books on Vedas were referred and presented here in a simple manner for all types of readers. I thank profusely my enterprising and illustrious friend Sri V.S. Narayan Rao, of Sri Pejavara Matha, for his encouragement with ideas, hints and moral back up. I also thank Sri Prasanth and Sri Hari who escorted me to the Neelavara Goshala along with the revered Swamiji. I thank Sri. L. Srinivasamurthy for initial DTP Works and Sri. K. Ganapathy Bhat, Vidhwan, Sri Pejavara Matha, Chennai for fine tuning the fine DTP presentation and conversion into a neat Garland of Flowers, page after page for printing perfection.

I thank once again His Holiness Pujyashree Vishvesha Theertha Swamiji and Sri Vishwaprasanna Theertha Swamiji without whose blessings this venture could not have been materialized.

S. Chakrapani

* * * * *

Preface

Are you a Cow lover? Then read this.

As human beings, everyone must identify themselves as a part and parcel of the society. They must volunteer towards the welfare of the people & society.'

So intimate is the cow's association with the lives of Hindus, that in all the rites of passage of life, from our Mother's conception to our cremation, or any ceremony, Pujas to Pithrukarya, Homas to Havana, Grahapravesam to Grahalakshmi, Panchakavya to make us pure, festivals to food, from coffee to any beverages, Holy Cow Gomatha is connected and is an integral part and intrinsic factor for anybody's life, children, parents, grandchildren, forefathers, future generations, pithrus and for all family celebrations.

Lord Krishna Avathara is a mission to save & protect the Cows & Bhagawat Bhakthas and if you believe, you are a pratibhimba of the Srishti starting from Sri Chaturmukha Brahma, continue the mission of "Go Samrakshana"

* * * * *

Introduction

"Soon after birth, all of us are fed by our Mother's breast milk upto 2 years. From 3rd year onwards, and even while she does not have adequate milk; cow assumes the role of our mother and feeds us until we breathe the last, till our last journey by her milk. Only from this milk, we get Curd, Butter, Buttermilk and Ghee. She is rightly called as "Gowmatha". Hence we must admit "We have two mothers"

"A help in need is always a help indeed"

"A voice from voiceless"

Experience divine grace by caring/helping destitute/deranged and down- trodden. All those who are born, until their death, one way or the other way, they carry on their task, just to satisfy their stomach. But that is not considered and counted as worthy of life.

One who, apart from his own life, makes others thrive happily, is aptly called "Noble life of a person" says **"Sri Vishvesha Theertha Swamiji"**

_____

Cows Anatomy / Cow – Human Genome Comparison

"Scientific America", a leading magazine has given a complete Cow Human Genome comparison. Among the 768 genes on the cattle RH map, 687 genes or 89.5% had putative human orthologs. Among the 687 mapped genes, 548 genes had human GB4 RH mapping information. 22 were mapped exclusively on the G3 panel and 68 had human cytogenetic assignments exclusively.

All cow chromosomes with the possible exception of BTA9 and BTA23 have centromere repositioning relative to human chromosomes. Four cattle chromosomes show complete conservation of synteny with their human homolog. The four are: BTA12 and HSA13, BTA19 and HSA17, BTA24 and HSA18, BTAX and HSAX. For all of these chromosomes multiple rearrangements were observed. BTA3 was the only cow chromosome that showed no internal rearrangements when compared with the homologous segment on HSA1. Fifteen cattle chromosomes are seen to be comprised of genes found on only one human chromosome.

Cow milk is the most compatible with human mother's milk than any other species in existence. This is because the DNA of the cow was specifically constructed to be harmonious with mammalian human DNA. So it can be clearly understood that cow DNA was designed so that humans could benefit from cows products being milk, cheese, butter, cream and yoghurt.

This knowledge is highly esoteric and confidential and incomprehensible to those outside the purview of the Vedic culture. It can only be known by that segment of society that is spiritually developed enough to completely abstain from all animal killing and flesh eating while understanding that the soul is eternal and exists in all living beings.

*****

Everybody Has Two Mothers.

Greatness of cow is spoken well in all Hindu scripts. Expenses covered for homas and yagnas may be high and elaborate. But a simple Gopooja is comparatively economical and at the same time fetches scintillating results say the experienced elders. Ox is said to be our father and cow is our dear mother.

Many cannot wake up without a bed coffee. Many cannot do their routine works without a single chaya (tea). Many cannot healthily attend to their karmas without 2 cups of milk. So, from early morning to bed , the cow's milk guides us, safeguards us and is a shouldering partner to add vigor and power for execution of our works. But these human beings do not care to see what happens to these cows, which are motherly companions. They keep quiet as silent spectators for all the ill happenings to this innocent and sacrificing creature. Everybody has two mothers. But many do not realize it.

Yes. Cows are the mothers of the universe. The human infant is fed breast milk by its human mother for less than three years. After weaning, the cow acts as the surrogate mother providing milk for the rest of the human life-through childhood, adult age and old age. Cow is verily the mother of the world. One would be filled with repugnance at the ungrateful idea of killing mother, whether surrogate mother or otherwise.

The cow is considered sacred in Hinduism. She is Go-Matha, the one who should be worshipped for the various graces she bestows on humanity.

The Hindu legends invariably treat the cow as sacred. Even some of the Muslim kings who ruled India, decided to impose a ban on their subjects eating beef as it was considered offensive to the majority Hindus who revered the cow. Fair.

* * * * *

Hinduism on Cows

Should one eat an animal that a substantial chunk of the population considers as sacred?

In Hinduism, the cow is considered sacred.

Most Hindus respect the cow for her docile, tolerant nature which exemplifies the cardinal virtue of Hinduism, non-injury, known as ahimsa.

The cow also symbolizes dignity, strength, endurance, maternity and selfless service.

Hindus worship the cow and it holds an honored place in society, and most Hindus do not eat beef. By honoring this gentle animal that gives more than it takes, Hindus honor all creatures.

In Hinduism, the cow is a symbol of wealth, strength, abundance, selfless giving and a full Earthly life. To the Hindu, the cow symbolizes all other creatures. Hindus regard all living creatures as sacred-mammals, fishes, birds. The cow is more a symbol of the Earth. It is the nourished, the ever-giving, undemanding provider, representing life and the support of life.

Honoring the cows instills in people, the virtues of gentleness, receptivity and connectedness with nature. The cow takes nothing but water, grass and grain, while it gives of its milk, as does the liberated soul give of his spiritual knowledge.

In the Hindu tradition, the cow is honored, garlanded and given special feedings at festivals all over India, most importantly the annual Gopashtama festival. Its nature is represented in Kamadhenu, the divine, wish-fulfilling cow. In India, more than 3,000 institutions called Gaushalaas, maintained by charitable trusts, care for old and infirm cows. The gift of a cow is applauded as the highest kind of gift.

"One can measure the greatness of a nation and its moral progress by the way it treats its animals. Cow protection to me is not mere protection of the cow. It means protection of all that lives and is helpless and weak in the world. The cow means the entire subhuman world" said Mahatma Gandhi.

"The cows have come and have brought us good fortune. In our stalls, contended, may they stay! May they bring forth calves for us, many-colored, giving milk for India each day! You make, O cows, the thin man sleek; to the unlovely you bring beauty. Rejoice our homestead with pleasant lowing. In our assemblies we laud your vigor." Rig Veda (4.28.1; 6) In the Rig Veda, cows represent wealth and joyous Earthly life. Several hymns refer to greatness of cattle.

* * * * *

Why do Hindus regard the Cow as Sacred?

We cannot give away anything unless a sure that it comes back to us. A few years ago in Madras an American devotee said to me, "Shall I give to the beggar who is asking?"

I said, "Give him ten rupees. You may need the fifty rupees, just as he needs the ten rupees now and this good deed, the karma, will pay you back more than what you give now. The karmic law pays higher interest than any bank when you give freely with no strings attached".

Rhetorical question: "Who is the greatest giver on planet earth today?" Who do we see on every table? What do we see in breakfast, lunch and dinner in every country of the world?

It is the Cow!!!!!!

The Golden Arches made millions out of cows. Popular companies have opened many cow-vending machines all over the world.

The generous cow gives milk and cream, yogurt and cheese, butter and ice cream, ghee, buttermilk, sirloin, ribs, rump, quarter round, porterhouse, beef stew. Its bones are the base for soup broths. It gives us our leather belt, leather seats, leather coats and shoes, beef jerky, cowboy hats, you name it. The cow is the most prominent **giving animal** in the world today.

And now the question: Why do the Hindus regard the cow as sacred?

Answer#1: People who ask if cows are considered sacred should understand that Hindus regard all living creatures as sacred-mammals, fishes, birds and more. The cow symbolically represents all other creatures to the Hindu.

Answer#2: The cow represents life and the sustenance of life to the Hindu. It represents our soul, our obstinate intellect, our unruly emotions, but the cow supersedes us because it is so giving, taking

13

nothing but grass and grain. It gives and gives and gives, as does the soul give and give and give.

Answer#3: The cow is so vital to life, the virtual sustainer of life for humans. In a society if you only had cows and no other domestic animals or agricultural pursuits, you could still survive and the children could survive with the butter, the cream and the milk to feed the children. The cow is a complete ecology, a gentle creature and a symbol of abundance.

Yes, the cow is considered very sacred in our religion and for very good reason. Its good qualities are those that we can emulate.

* * * * *

Why Cow is Sacred?

The reason why Hindus worship cows is an enigma for most non-Hindus. They cannot understand why we would want to worship one of the most docile animals in the world. Lions, eagles and dragons they can understand, but a cow!?! Hindus have worshiped cows since the earliest time in our civilization. Our earliest prayers invoke the Almighty to look after our cattle and make sure it's never sick or stolen. Its propagation and preservation has been one of the main aims of our social duties since the time of the Vedas.

WHY? Like all societies of all times, we, the Hindus, have hoarded what we have considered to be "wealth". Whether it's measured in stones (jades, diamonds) metals (gold, silver, bronze), skins/furs, feathers (quetzal feathers in South America), shells, silks, weapons or animals (elephants, cows), wealth is wealth. Cows were a measure of wealth. They still are in many parts of the world. Cows provide milk which helps sustain life, life of adults and children alike. The by-products of the milk, yoghurt, buttermilk, butter etc., are an integral part of their daily diet. Their dung was a free, useful, year-round fuel supply. Being tame, they are an excellent beast of burden. By pulling carts and ploughs, they are partners in technology that helped develop new frontiers in the Indian sub-continent.

Even after death, their skins are useful in various ways. Their usefulness meant they were valued as highly as any treasure of gold, gem or sometimes even kin. Due to its multi-purpose usefulness, cows became a "good luck charm". If a cow passed you, it was considered to be good luck. In scholarly books, this is referred to as auspicious, but it only means lucky! If a black cat can be interpreted as bad luck in 21st century Europe, why can't a cow be considered as lucky in modern India?

How can you guarantee that this valuable resource is not abused, or mistreated by society at large? By giving it a very special place in our society, that of a pseudo mother, we made sure it was respected at all times. By giving it the same respectful status as a "parent", the ancients made sure the humble cow had the same legal and social protection as humans! All this is to protect their/our wealth!! With time, other modes of wealth took greater precedence than the cow. Milk and dung were still an essential to the rural masses, but, the cow stopped being the object wealth. Rituals still required milk and its by-products, especially when Hinduism became more vegetarian. As a result, the spiritual overtones cow' "divine" status became even more ingrained in the social psyche.

* * ** *

The Srimad Bhagavad-Gita and the Sacredness Of Cows

Lord Krishna states in Srimad Bhagavad-Gita: Chapter 10, verse 28 dhenunam asmi kamadhuk

Dhenunam-among cows, asmi-I am, kamadhuk-the wish fulfilling cow. Among the cows I am the wish fulfilling cow.

In this verse Lord Krishna reveals that amongst the cows He is manifested as the Kamadhuk meaning Kamadhenu the original wish fulfilling cows known as the Surabhi Cows. Just who and what are the Surabhi cows and how the Surabhi Cows attained such an elevated and exalted position that they are able to represent a portion of the energy of the supreme Lord Krishna will be revealed in the following information given in the Anusasana Parva of the Mahabharata by Krishna Dvaipayana Vyasa.

The Surabhi Cow descended from the spiritual worlds and manifested herself in the heavenly spheres from the aroma of celestial nectar for the benefit of all created beings. The direct descendants of the Surabhi cows are the sacred cows from the continent India which are uniquely distinguished the same as the Surabhi by the beautiful hump on their backs and the wonderfully soft folds of skin under their necks.

Since all cows in existence in the world today are factual descendants of the sacred cows of India they are all holy as well and should always be lovingly cared for and protected with the highest esteem and greatest respect. One should never cause harm to cows in any way even in a dream and one should never ever even think of eating the flesh of cows as there is no action more sinful in all of creation then cow killing.

Cows are the mothers of all creatures. Cows are verily the mothers of the 33 crores of demigods that administrate creation in the material existence throughout all the universes. Cows are the goddesses of the gods and the refuge of all auspiciousness. Cows bestow every kind of happiness and for these reason they always are worship able. Cows are the support of all the worlds for by their milk they nourish terrestrial beings and by their ghee offered in sacrifice they nourish the denizens of the celestial realms. Nothing is superior to cows.

A cow should not be owned by one who is a killer of cows or a seller to killers of cows, by one who is unrighteous, by one who is sinful, by one who is untruthful in speech, and by one who is outside of the Vedic culture nor should cows ever be given to one such as these. Gifts of cows should be made after ascertaining and determining the qualification of the receiver. Cows should never be given unto those whose residence they are likely to suffer from fire or sun. Cows should always be given away accompanied by their calves. Those cows that have been rescued from situations of distress or have been received from humble farmers unable to continue to take care of them properly are considered to be most auspicious.

One should never show disrespect for cows in any way nor should one feel any repugnance towards the urine and dung of a cow because these things are also pure. When cows are grazing or laying down relaxing one should never disturb or annoy them in any way. Cows should never be killed in any type of sacrifice or slaughtered in any way for food as the killing of cows constitutes the most heinous of all sins in existence.

Cows are the foremost of all creatures in all the worlds. It is from cows that the means for sustaining the worlds has established. Cows are auspicious and sacred and the bequeathed of every blessing! Cows benefit humans with milk, yoghurt, cheese butter and ghee. The Vedas have stated that the milk of a cow is equivalent to ambrosial nectar and that ghee derived from cow's milk is the best of all libations poured onto the sacred fires of Brahmins.

Cows of various kinds and diverse colors are always to be worshiped. They are the foremost, of all creatures existing in this universe. Morning and evening one should bow one's head in reverence to cows. One should never show any disregard to cows in any way but should always show them respect. When one awakes in the morning one should always remember cows. Before falling to sleep at night one should always remember cows.

Cows are always auspicious.

Cows are also fragrant. The wonderful scent of the amities agallochum emanates from out of their sacred bodies.

Cows are the great refuge of all creatures. Cows constitute the greatest sources of blessings for all creatures. Cows are the past. Cows are the future. Cows are the source of evolution and eternal growth. Cows are the root of prosperity. Whatever is given to cows always produces good fortune and is never in vain. It is solely and exclusively from the ghee of cows that the sacred rituals prescribed and authorized in the Vedas is empowered and able to be performed.

Without the presence of cows ghee there is no possibility of performing sacred rituals that will gratify the 33 million demigods who are responsible for universal management.

Neither will the Supreme Personality of Godhead, Lord Krishna be pleased and satisfied. Ghee comes exclusively only from cows from whom flow offerings of milk and milk products. Thus cows verily establish the purity of all sacred rituals and constitute the very essence of performing all sacred activities being the very source of sacred activities.

Cows represent sacred acts themselves and without cows there can be no performance of any sacred act. This is the pure, sublime and supremely exalted position and pre-eminence of cows above all creatures in all the worlds.

One who knows the pre-eminence of cows and the selfless service cows render to all creatures and does not protect them affectionately is a sinner and offender and their destination is certainly hell. Cows are equal to the rays of the sun that travel through the universe giving light, warmth and nourishment.

In previous yugas the Vedic injunction was given jiyaite pare yadi tabe mare prani veda-purane ache ajna vane that means in the Vedic scriptures known as Puranas there are injunctions declaring that one can take the life of a living being only if they are able to revive it back to life again by chanting Vedic mantras. But we find that this injunction has been terminated in today's age of kaliyuga by the Brahma-Vaivarta Purana where it is stated that in the present age of kali Yuga it is forbidden to kill cows under any circumstances.

Cows are equivalent to our mothers for when the mother's milk has dried up the cow gives her milk unselfishly to nourish and strengthen us. How can one who has ever drunken cow's milk justify the killing and eating of such a mother as the sacred cow?

One should never even in one's mind do injury to a cow or ever think of harming cows as well as bulls. One should show all respect and compassion for cows and sincere reverence should be offered unto them all without reservation.

Those who fail to give cows reverence and protection and choose to foolishly oppose and whimsically ignore the injunctions of the Vedic scriptures by selling a cow for slaughter, by killing a cow, by eating cows flesh and by permitting the slaughter of cows will all rot in the darkest regions of hell for as many thousands of years as there are hairs on the body of each cow slain. There is no atonement for the killing of a cow.

Go-ange yata loma tata sahasra vatsara

Go-vadhi raurava-madhye pace nirantar

Cow killers and cow eaters are condemned to rot in hell for as many thousands of years as there are for each hair on the body of every cow they eat from.

In comparison to the contrary, sanctified living beings with purified souls that make gifts of cows to worthy twice born in the three higher ashrams established in the Vedas attain celestial realms for as many years as there are hairs upon the body of the cows given away in charity. There is no gift higher in merit than the gift of cows to a Vaishnava or duly initiated brahmana of the Vedic culture in one of the four authorized sampradayas.

Cows constitute the highest good. Cows are the root of great blessings for all living beings. Cows are the source of eternal growth. Cows are the past and the future. Evolution itself depends upon cows. The mantras used for Vedic rituals such as Swaha and Vashat without which no Vedic rites are complete are eternally established in cows. Cows verily are the fruit of all Vedic rituals because all Vedic rituals are dependent upon the ghee from cows form the performance of sacred rituals which benefit all of creation. Thus the protection of cows is the greatest dharma or eternal duty for all living beings.

There is no wealth that is equal to cows. To talk about cows, to hear others speak about cows, to offer gifts of cows to worthy people and to see cows are all auspicious activities. There is never any inauspiciousness in cows. On Earth cows represent high energy and are endued with the elements of strength and energetic exertion. There are also elements of great wisdom in cows and they are the givers of great happiness upon all creatures. The country or nation where cows are protected and live without fear of slaughter becomes exalted and the sins of that country are evaporated. Cows constitute the stairs that lead to heaven. Cows are adored in heaven. Cows are goddesses competent to grant every righteous wish and desire. Verily there is nothing in the worlds more elevated or superior to cows.

Cows are superior to all yogis and ascetics and because of this liberated divine being perform their austerities in the company and presence of cows. Cows do not feel cold or heat nor can rain afflict. Cows are never to be sacrificed they are to be given as gifts to worthy Brahmanas. The ruler who gives gifts of cows to the foremost of Brahmanas is sure to overcome every calamity he encounters. It is ordained in the eternal Vedas that ghee from the cow is the best of all ingredients offered as libations into the sacrificial fire.

For this reason one who makes a gift of a cow to worthy Brahmnas who will then use the ghee from this cow to perform Vedic ceremonies, that fortunate gifter is regarded as making a gift of a libation for sacrifice. A bovine bull is considered to be the embodiment of heaven. One who offers a bovine bull to an accomplished brahmana has factually reserved themselves a place in heaven.

Cows that have been rescued and protected and cared for in distress give even more merit as well as cows received from persons in distress due to an inability to properly take care of their cows.

A cow must never be given to a tiller of soil. Only a bovine bull may be given to a tiller of soil but never a cow. Neither a cow nor a bull should ever be given unto one who will kill them. Nor should a cow or a bull be given unto an atheist or one who makes a business selling or trading cows.

The Vedas have stated that one who gives away cows or bulls to such sinful persons suffers interminably in a hellish condition.

To the Hindu, the cow symbolizes all other creatures. Hindus regard all living creatures as sacred-mammals, fishes, birds. The cow is more, a symbol of the Earth. It is the nourisher, the ever-giving, undemanding provider, representing life and the support of life.

There is no gift that is higher in merit than the gift of cows. A cow lawfully acquired if given away in charity protects the whole dynasty of the giver. Cows are the source of that immortality which Vedic sacrifices prescribe. They have within them the nature of both the sun and the moon. Cows verily constitute and determine the eternal destiny of creation.

Cows are the life breath of all living creatures therefore one who makes a gift of a cow is said to be making a gift of life breath of all living creatures. Cows are also constituted as the great refuge of all living creatures thus one who makes a gift of a cow is said to be making a gift of that which is the great refuge of all living creatures.

When the Surabhi cows first manifested from the aroma of ambrosial nectar they performed severe penance for 1,00,000 years for the purpose of acquiring the spiritual merit to be the foremost of all things needed for the performance of Vedic rituals and ceremonies; thus only from cow milk exclusively is sanctified ghee produced for the performance of Vedic rituals.

Whatever is produced from any and all other types of milk is not authorized by Vedic scriptures and thus not being sanctioned by the Vedas can never be used in any Vedic rituals or ceremonies.

At the conclusion of the Surabhi cows are austerities Brahma himself appeared before them and granted their wishes blessing them with the benediction that cows would eternally be the sustainers of all creatures. This is why cows are sacred and most holy and the foremost of all creatures in creation and verily the refuge of all the worlds.

The cow is extremely important regarding the destiny of the total human species in all the worlds and creation itself that her value is impossible to overestimate. The name for cow in the Vedas is known as aghyna which means inviolable. Another name is ahi which means not to be killed and another is aditi which means never to be cut into pieces.

* * * * *

Go Pooja and Cow Worship

Magnificent but simple, humble, quiet and salient qualities have made it a worshipping creature on this vast earth. The Vedas and purana firmly stress that Lord and Lordess reside in its physical structure and shower various fortunes, bliss and eternal happiness who worship it with faith and belief.

It is said in Purana that king Dilipan worshiped and performed Gopooja (cow worship) and attained all prosperity and greatness. Instead of performing hundreds and hundreds of Poojas, homas, yagnas and many rituals, one can kill his past sins and achieve his desire fulfilled by just doing Gopooja say the puranas & Vedas.

What a wonderful act it should be to replace all great homas & yagnas? What a brilliant creation it should be? A simple Gopooja has enormous power and sanctity to offer multimillion richness, blessings and well being. Of course a worship to cow is nothing but worshipping of various deities residing in it in different forms.

Hence the net result of worshipping a single cow pleases all the deities like Lord Vishnu, Lord Shiva, Lord Brahma, Lordess Lakshmi, Lordess Parvati, Lordess Saraswathi and various Maharishis and Devatas reside in it. You need not run after kshetras, temples and temples in various nook and corner of this world.

You can simply achieve whatever you wish; whatever sin you wish to wash off; whatever you wish to acquire; whatever wealth you wish to attain; whatever, well being you are running after; by just worshipping a cow, say the Vedas.

Gorakshana (feeding a cow) also offer unique benefits in one's life.

Cow and bull worship was a common practice in many parts of the world, beginning in Mesopotamia around 6,000 B.C. and spreading to Northwestern India with the invasion of the Indus Valley in the second millennium B.C. by Aryan nomadic pastoralists who established the

Vedic religion. What is remarkable is that such worship has persisted uniquely in India to the present day.

It is concluded that revulsion against sacrifice, the economic usefulness of cattle and religious symbolism (especially as the Mother-provider) were factors contributing to the formulation of the sacred cow doctrine, but it was ahimsa (the principle of non-violence/ non-harming) that provided the moral and ethical compulsion for the doctrine's widespread acceptance in later Indian religious though and social behavior.

When we build a new house then we celebrate a function called "Nuthana Grahapravesa" making an entry into the new built house in an auspicious way on an auspicious day. To perform this function we consult an astrologer to fix an auspicious day.

The astrologer usually demands the horoscope of house owner's wife for fixing the day, date and time for Grahapravesha function and for special poojas since she is the Grahalakshmi. The husband, even though he has invested several lakhs, is totally sidelined and forgotten. Money has no value in this great function.

Secondly on that day, for performing all homas like Vaasthu Navagraha Homa, and Ganapathy homas, the priest will say that the husband and wife will have the qualification and right to enter the house only after performing Gowpuja. The cow and its calf have to enter the house first. Then in serial order the wife (Grahalakshmi), has to enter and then only the husband will enter.

In olden days in every village and household, the women soon after their bath will first do Gowpooja by applying thilak to the cows or to the picture of cows in the pooja rooms. Here also Cow occupies a prime position of top priority.

Even in the wall pictures of Sri Raghavendra Swamy, we can see him with a cow (Kamadenu). The most popular sloka also says "Poojyaya Raghavendraya Sathyadharma rathayacha bajatham kalpavrikshaya namatham kamadenave". The slokas says that he is like kamadenu giver of all benefits, fortunes and blessings. When the cows are pleased keshava residing in them is satisfied. "Tasya pranyupakarenu prito Bhavati Keshava".

During Hindu marriage as part of one major important function during the day the bridegroom takes the hands of the bride and takes 7 steps for harmony and prosperity after marriage. During the 5th step the mantra says that the Lord Vishnu come with you to bless you with wealth in cattle (Cow).

Hence it is crystal clear that wealth comes through cows only.

The ladies during the 'Chaturmasa' adhere to Gopadamam vrata (a disciplined way of living with devotion). This will wipe out all sins, fear of diseases and free from hell say the holy Hindu scripts and Vedas. In that they draw the figure of a cow and perform the necessary Poojas. This once again reveals the greatness of cows for happy and trouble free life on earth.

* * * * *

Quotes from Holy Scriptures

In the Rig Veda X.87.16 we find: "One who partakes of human flesh, the flesh of a horse or of another animal and deprives others from milk by slaughtering cows; if such a fiend does not desist then even cut off their heads by your powers , Oh King".

"The cows have come and have brought us good fortune. In our stalls, contented, may they stay! May they bring forth calves for us, many-colored, giving milk for Indra each day? You make, O cows, the thin man sleek; to the unlovely you bring beauty. Rejoice our homestead with pleasant lowing. In our assemblies we laud your vigor." Rig Veda (4:28.1; 6) In the Rig Veda, cows represent wealth and joyous Earthly life. Several hymns refer to ten thousand and more cattle.

In the Atharvana Veda VIII.6.23 we find: Those who eat cooked or uncooked flesh, who eat eggs and embryos are following an evil addiction that must be put to an end. In the Srimad Bhagavatam, Canto 11, chapter 5, verse 14 we find; Those who are ignorant of the absolute truth and believe they are virtuous although wicked and arrogant who kill animals without any feeling of remorse or fear of punishment are devoured by those very same animals in their next birth.

In the Mahabharata, Anusasana-parva, 115.43-116.45 we find: That wretch among men, who pretending to follow the path of righteousness prescribed in the Vedas, would kill living creatures from greed of flesh would certainly go to hellish regions. In the Manu-samhita, chapter 4, verse 162 we find: A guru, a teacher, a father, a mother, a brahmana, a cow and a yogi all should never be killed.

Even in the Old Testament of the Bible which applies to both Christians and Jews in Issaih, chapter 66 verse 3 we find: He that killeth an ox is as if he slew a man. He that sacrifices a lamb is as if he slit a dogs neck, he that offereth it is an oblation is as if he offered swines blood, he that burneth it is incense as if he blessed an idol. Yea they have chosen their way and their soul delighteth in their abominations".

In the Mahabharata, Anusasana-parva, 114.6, 115.6 it states: As the footprints of all moving, living beings are engulfed in those of the elephant, even thus all religions are to be understood by ahimsa which is non-violence to any living being by thought, words or actions.

So from these examples it can be clearly understood that cow killing and cow eating were definitely not sanctioned by the Vedic scriptures to the contrary they were condemned; and also according to the authority of the Bible cow killing is not sanctioned in the Christian religion either.

* * * * *

Tirumandiram/Lingaya Vachanas/ Sandilya Upanishad/ Thirukural

Let your aims be common, and your hearts be of one accord, and all of you be of one mind, so you may live well together. Rig Veda Samhita 10.191

Protect both our species, two-legged and four-legged with both food and water for their needs. May they with us increase in stature and strength! Save us from hurt all our days, O Powers1 Rig Veda Samhita 10.37.11 VE, 319

One who partakes of human flesh, the flesh of a horse or of another animal, and deprives others of milk by slaughtering cows, O king, if such a fiend does not desist by other means, and then you should not hesitate to cut off his head/Rig Veda Samhita, 10.87.16, FS 90

Peaceful be the earth, peaceful the ether, peaceful the heaven, peaceful the waters, peaceful the herbs, peaceful the trees. May all Gods bring me peace! May there be peace through these invocations of peace. With these invocations of peace which appease everything, I render peaceful whatever here is terrible; whatever here is cruel, whatever here is sinful. Let it become auspicious; let everything be beneficial to us. Atharva Veda Samhita 10.191.4

Those noble souls who practice meditation and other yogic ways, who are ever careful about all beings, who protect all animals, are the ones who are actually serious about spiritual practices / Atharva Veda Samhita 19.48.5 FS,90

If we have injured space, the earth or heaven, or if we have offended mother or father, from that may Agni, fire of the house, absolve us and guide us safely to the world of goodness/Atharva Veda Samhita 6.120.1. VE, 636.

You must not use your God-given body for killing God's creatures, whether they are human, animal or whatever. Yajur Veda Samhita 12.32.

FS, 90 May all beings look at me with a friendly eye. May I do likewise, and may we all look on each other with the eyes of a friend / Yajur Veda 36.18.

Nonviolence is all the offerings. Renunciation is the priestly honorarium. The final purification is death. Thus all the Divinities are established in this body. Krishna Yajur Veda, Prana Upanishad 46-8. VE, 413-14

To the heavens be peace, to the sky and the earth; to the waters be peace, to plants and all trees; to the Gods be peace, to Brahman be peace to all men be peace, again and again-peace also to me! Oh! Earthen vessel, strengthen me. May all beings regard me with friendly eyes! May I look upon all creatures with friendly eyes! With a friend's eye may we regard each other! Shukla Yajur Veda Samhita 36.17-18. VE, 306; 342

No pain should be caused to any created being or thing / Devikalottara agama, JAV 69-79.RM, 116

Mahabharata and Bhagvad Gita, Epic History

The very name of the cows is aghnya, indicating that they should never be slaughtered. Who then could slay them? Surely, one who kills a cow or a bull commits the most heinous crime. Mahabharata, Shantiparva 262.47. FS, PG.94

The purchaser of flesh performs himsa (violence) by his wealth; he who eats flesh does so by enjoying its taste; the killer does himsa by actually tying and killing the animal. Thus, there are three forms of killing: he who brings flesh or sends for it, he who cuts off the limbs of an animal, and he who purchase, sells or cooks flesh and eats it-all of these are to be considered meat-eaters-Mahabharata, ANU.115.40. FS, PG 90

He who desires to augment his own flesh by eating the flesh of other creatures lives in misery in whatever species he may take his birth-Mahabharata, ANU.115.47. FS, PG.90

One should never do that to another which one regards as injurious to one's own self. This, in brief, is the rule of dharma. Yielding to desire and acting differently, one becomes guilty of adharma. Mahabharata 18.113.8

Those high-souled persons who desire beauty, faultlessness of limbs, long life, understanding, mental and physical strength and memory should abstain from acts of injury-Mahabharata 18.115.8.

Ahimsa is the highest dharma. Ahimsa is the best tapas. Ahimsa is the greatest gift. Ahimsa is the highest self-control. Ahimsa is the highest sacrifice. Ahimsa is the highest power. Ahimsa is the highest friend. Ahimsa is the highest truth. Ahimsa is the highest teaching - Mahabharata 18.116.37.41

He who sees that the Lord of all is ever the same in all that is-immortal in the field of mortality-he sees the truth. And when a man sees that the God in himself is the same God in all that is, he hurts not himself by hurting others. Then he goes, indeed, to the highest path-Bhagvad Gita 13.27-28. BGM, PG.101

Nonviolence, truth, freedom from anger, renunciation, serenity, aversion to fault- finding, sympathy for all beings, peace from greedy cravings, gentleness, modesty, steadiness, energy, forgiveness, fortitude, purity, a good will, freedom from pride these belong to a man who is born for heaven. Bhagvad Gita 16.2-3. BGM, PG.109

Tirumandiram and Other Scriptures: Many are the lovely flowers of worship offered to the Guru, but none lovelier than non-killing. Respect for life is the highest worship, the bright lamp, the sweet garland and unwavering devotion-Tirumantiram 197

Spiritual Merit and sin are our own making. The killer of other lives is an outcast. Match your words with your conduct. Steal not, kill not, indulge not in self-praise condemn not others to their face-Lingayat Vachanas

Ahimsa is not causing pain to any living being at any time through the actions of one's mind, speech or body-Sandilya Upanishad. When mind stuff is firmly based in waves of ahimsa, all living beings cease their enmity in the presence of such a person. Yoga Sutras 2.35. YP, PG.205

Those who are ignorant of real dharma and though wicked and haughty, account themselves virtuous, kill animals without any feeling of remorse or fear of punishment. Further, in their next lives, such sinful persons will be eaten by the same creatures they have killed in this world-Shrimad Bhagavatam 11.5.4 FS, PG.90

The Tirukural, Preeminent Ethical Scripture: Perhaps nowhere is the principle of nonmeat-eating so fully and eloquently expressed as in the Tirukural, written in the Tamil language by a simple weaver saint in a village near Madras over 2,000 years ago. Considered the worlds' greatest ethical scripture, it is sworn on in South Indian courts of law. It is the principle of the pure in heart never to injure others, even when they themselves have been hatefully injured. What is virtuous conduct? It is never destroying life, for killing leads to every other sin-312; 321, TW

Harming others, even enemies who harmed you unprovoked, assures incessant sorrow. The supreme principle is this. Never knowingly harm anyone at any time in any way-313; 317, TW

What is the good way? It is the path that reflects on how it may avoid killing any living creature. Refrain from taking precious life from any living being, even to save your own life-324; 327, TW

Riches cannot be found in the hands of the thriftless. Nor can compassion be found in the hearts of those who eat meat-TK 252, TW

Goodness is never one with the minds of these two: one who wields a weapon and one who feasts on a creature's flesh-TK 253, TW

If you ask, "What is kindness and what is unkind? It is not killing and killing. Thus, eating flesh is never virtuous"-TK 254, TW

Life is perpetuated by not eating meat. The clenched jaws of hell hold those who do. TK 255, TW

If the world did not purchase and consume meat, there would be none to slaughter and offer meat for sale-TK 256, TW

When a man realizes that meat is the butchered flesh of another creature, he must abstain from eating it-TK 257, TW

Perceptive souls who have abandoned passion will not feed on flesh abandoned by life-TK 258, TW

Greater than a thousand ghee offerings consumed in sacrificial fires is to not sacrifice and consume any living creature - TK 259, TW

All that lives will press palms together in prayerful adoration of those who refuse to slaughter and savor meat-TK 260, TW

Hindu Scriptures on Eating Meat/Killing Animals

The Hindu scriptures from the oldest Vedic to all the later layers in time all advocate vegetarianism and not killing animals and certainly never offer animals in their Yajnas!

The Vedic word frequently mentioned is Aghnya=not to be killed. This word was in particular used for cows.

Aahavaniiye maamsapratishedha (Katyayana Sutra)

That which is used in Yajna (Aahavaniiya) must be vegetarian

Maa himsyaat sarvabhuutaani. (Rig Veda)

No creature/animal should be killed.

Yah paurusheyena kravishaa samankte yo ashvyena pashunaa yaatudhaanah, Yo aghyaayaa bharati kshiiramagne teshaam shirshaani harasaapi vrshcha. (RV 10.87.16)

The evil person who kills or eats the meat of a horse or cow deserves to be terminated.

Dhaanaa dhenurabhavad, vatso'syaastilo'bhavat. (Atharva Veda 18.4.32) Rice is named as 'cow' and sesame a 'calf'. [Just like someone saying 'I want the meat of hazel=I want the nut of hazel]

Maamsapaakapratishedhashcha tadvat. (Miimaamsa Suutra 10.3.65)

Killing and eating meat is totally prohibited.

Dhenuvachcha ashvadakshinaa. (MS 10.3.65)

Like a cow is given (in charity) so also a horse.

Suraam matsyaan madhu maamsamaasavam krsaraudanam, Dhuurttaih pravartitam hyetannaitad vedashu kalpitam. (Mahabharata, Shaanti Parva 265.9)

It is only the evil-minded hypocrites who started telling that Vedic Yajnas involve intoxicants and meat eating. It is not in the Vedas. [This comment must have been around the time, far beyond the Bharata Battle and in post-Vedic times, when many customs arrived in the Vedic Heartland, which were totally foreign to its culture]

The full Anushaasana Parva of the Mahaabhaaratam discusses the evils of meat eating: Akhaadannanumodamshcha bhaavadoshena maanavah, Yo'numodati hanyantam so'pi doshena lipyate. (MB, Anushaasana Parva 115.39)

The one who himself doesn't eat meat but even if he gives his consent to eat meat or to kill an animal, he becomes equally sinful as them.

Ijyaayajnashrutikrtairyaa maargairabudho' dhamah, Hanyaajjantuun maamsagradhnuh sa vai narakabhaangnarah. (MB, AP 115.43)

The meat-eater who kills an animal in the name of Vedic Yajna or tells that it is a requirement of the Yajna is a sinner and he will be a person who will dwell in hell.

Aahartaa chaanumantaa cha vishastaa krayavikrayii, Samskartaa chopabhoktaa cha khaadakaah sarva eva te. (MB, AP 115.45)

The one who brings an animal to be killed, the one who buys an animal to be killed, the one who sells, buys, cooks and eats the meat are all sinners.

Na dadyaadaamisham shraddhe na chaadyaad dharmatattvavit, munyannaiah, syaatparaa priitiryathaa na pashuhimsayaa. (Bhagavatam 7.15.7)

It is Dharma that in the Shraaddha feast he should never offer meat nor should eat meat. Only vegetarian food must be offered because meat is obtained by killing. [One can understand that in the days of this particular verse, the mainstream Hindus were confronted with people starting to eat meat]

Naitaadrshah paro dharmo nrnaam saddharmaamichehataam, nyaaso dandasya bhuuteshu manovaakkaayajasya yah. (Bhagavatam 7.15.8) This is the best Dharma to observe for everyone that one should not hurt other beings even in his thoughts.

* * * * *

Manu Smriti or Manava Dharma Shastra

Manu strongly admonishes that one should never drink and should never even smell any intoxicant like wine. (MS.11.146-149)

Manu asserts that selling, buying, cooking and eating meat is a sin which is as great as killing an animal itself. (MS5.15)

Gaudii Paishtii cha Maadhvii cha Vijneyaa trividhaa suraa. Yathaivaika tathaa sarvaa na paatavyaa dvijottamaih. (MS 11.94) yaksharakshah pishaachaannam madyam maamsam suraasavam. Tad braahmena naattavyam devaanaamashnataa havih. (MS 11.95)

Brahmans, kshatriyas and vaishyas should never drink wine, liquor or intoxicants of any kinds, because intoxicants, wine liquor and meat of animals are the food of Yakshas, Rakshasas and Pishachas (all kind of non-Vedic people or even demons). O they must not be consumed.

Naakrtvaa praaninaam himsaam maamsamutpadyate kvachit. Na cha praanivadhah svargyastamaanmaamsam vivarjayet. (MS 5.48) Anumantaa vishasitaa nihantaa krayavikrayii. Samskartaa chopahartaa cha khaadakashchetighaatakaah (MS 5.51)

Flesh of animals is obtained only after killing them, which is a sin, and the killer of animals never enters the celestial abode. All those involved in killing, consenting the killing, helping the killing, carrying, selling, buying, cooking and eating the meat of an animal are equally sinful as the killing of that animal.

Yatkimchinmadhusammishram gokshiiram ghrtapaayasam, dattamakshayamityaahuh pitarah puurvadevataah. (MP 17.36) Apart from the cow's milk, honey and the sweet pudding made of milk and rice and sugar with dry nuts satisfies Pitru forever.

* * * * *

Torture and Slaughter of Cows

Is it not a shameful attitude and disgraceful act on our part to be silent observers when these cows are butchered and tortured everywhere in India for the sake of cheap money and food?

Are we true citizens of India? Are we true followers of Hindu faith? Are we really noble men and women when these pathetic situations slash the poor cows?

We are totally going in a wrong path. We are treading a path of thorns when we ignore the tragedy happenings of the cows.

While going along the national highways, we can see minimum 30 cows dumped in a lorry and taken miles together without a sip of water, food and care. They are so badly dumped that they are unable to move its head or legs. What a tragedy?

More they dump more economical for them for transportation of cows. If the roads are bad, still more struggle and suffocation happens to them which tortures all along the way. Not more than 5 or 6 should be loaded on a single lorry, which should be loaded with grass, water and other required items for them. But do we see such an arrangement done for these cows?

It is a totally intolerable gesture done by merciless men who are after money they get from these sacred cows. Their milk, flesh skin fetch lakhs and lakhs of rupees. But they are uncared and savaged like cheap creations. No! No it is intolerable. Slash this! Stop this! Let rules & regulations come forward to put an end to this disgraceful gesture.

Let us see what is happening in the slaughter houses and in streets to the cows! Oh! Oh! Horrible! Disgraceful! Merciless!! Mind boggling scenes! Unbearable incorrigible tortures!

Are we Indians! Are we really true believer of non violence! Are we all stupid silent spectators of this violence to a very kind and very noble creature which looks after us and nurtures us from birth to end of our life?

Are we sensible! Are we not morally responsible for this butchering menace! Are we not responsible by not stopping this?

When a tiger is shot or hurt a big hue and cry is seen in parliament and in the press. When a lion is hunted even then a big scene is created amongst the elites. When a deer is hunted imprisonment and court orders are thrown on the individual whoever he may be.

But when a sacred Cow is tortured, butchered and battered no one raises a voice! No one issues notice! No one raises it in the parliament. No one writes it to the press. No one reports for legal action! No one is sensible enough to make a hue and cry for this noble cow! What a pity! What a disgrace! What a meaningless citizens? What an insipid rules & regulations? What a pathetic bloodshed activity it is, that nobody cares? Totally ignored murder! Totally lawless killing and torture!

From the 3 southern states alone, about 20 lakhs cattle are taken to Kerala every year for slaughter, where Beef is 40% staple food and the products are exported.

There are 7000 + unlicensed abattoirs in Kerala. The butchers for a fair price buy the cattle from calves, to milk animals including healthy bullocks.

These animals are tied by neck and made to walk without food or water for miles together, or transported in lorries with a single rope passing through their noses in tightly packed rows or bundled one over the other with their legs broken by iron rod.

Every cow is killed in full view of others waiting in horror. An iron pipe is inserted deep into the throat followed by a sharp iron rod to cut off the wind pipe and food pipe, and when the cow is struggling for breath and blood is gushing, lime water is pumped into the stomach to gain extra meat weight and then starts skinning while alive and cutting out other parts! (www.haindavakeralam.com).

By killing one animal, the benefits they derive are; Hide: Rs.3500 and above depending upon the animal

Beef : about 350 to 500 kgs @ Rs 70/kg

Blood and liver : sold to pharmaceutical companies

Bones : sold to sugar factories / pharmaceutical units

Bone marrow : sold to dog feed manufacturers

Fat: bought by detergent, oil, ghee manufactures.

**Before every milking, the cows and buffaloes are injected with a hormone 'Oxytocin', which cause immense uterus pain

**Nature has blessed the new calf with an enzyme "Rennet' to sustain in the initial days, but this is also sliced out from its stomach for manufacturing cheese.

**The cost of mutton and beef is Rs70 and 250 respectively, and hence largely adulterated.

**Due to indiscriminate mass slaughtering over the years 64 out of 96 swadesi Indian breeds have been totally wiped out.

**The laws to prevent cruelty to animals are in force in the states, but are largely ignored.

Example: Transport of cattle for slaughter is prohibited. For any other purpose, only 6 animals should be transported in a lorry-but 30 to 40 are transported.

**Certain acts like twisting tails; testicles etc are non-bailable offences punishable under sec.428/429 of IPC.

**No skinning or cutting should be done before the death is complete.

**On many occasions, even the cows given in 'Godhana' after the death of a Hindu is also sold ultimately to the butchers. At times, Cows offered to temples are also diverted for slaughter by the vested interests.

**Certain worms present in beef enter the human brain and proliferate and cause dangerous conditions viz. Neuron cysticercosis' which may prove fatal also.

**For manufacturing very expensive leather, a full pregnant cow is made to stand in a small cement tank, hot water is poured till tail level and some persons beat it with rods. Out of fear and gruesome treatment, the cow delivers and the fetus is pressed into the hot water and the skin of the calf is peeled out and processed in the same temperature. Also, the leather from 5 such cow's hide is said to be very soft and is used in the upholstery of one expensive car.

**These cows and buffaloes produce milk for their own calves like our own women. But, on most occasions, the calves are killed immediately after birth not only to rob the milk but also to capitalize on their skin and meat. Cows are extremely intelligent with a strong bondage for their calves. They can identify a beef-eater by smell when approached and feel uneasy while passing by a slaughter-house.

But, in our only land of Lord Sri Rama, Lord Krishna, the great Buddha, and Sri Madwacharya, even a few thousands of these cattle are not taken care of in their old age. The plight of the dry cows and the old cattle is miserable and are subjected to a lot of cruelty. Due to socio-economic reasons and ignorance, some sell these unproductive animals to butchers who in turn make hefty profits by selling their skin, meat, blood, liver and bones.

We the real beneficiaries of the stolen milk consciously are bound to protect these known mothers and help in providing a peaceful living.

Cattle slaughter

Except in West Bengal and Kerala, where cattle slaughter is permitted, the Cow Slaughter Act prohibits the killing of cattle less than 16 years of age. The penalty for illegal slaughter of cattle is rigorous imprisonment for two years and a fine. Article 48 of the Constitution of India, Part IV Directive Principles of State Policy, Articles 48-Organization of Agriculture and Animal Husbandry, says: "The State shall endeavor to organize agriculture and animal husbandry on modern and scientific lines and shall, in particular, take steps for preserving and improving the breeds and prohibiting the slaughter of cows and calves and other milk and draught cattle.

According to one government study, 50 percent of small animal slaughtering and 70 percent of large animal slaughtering is illegal, taking place in clandestine facilities where there is no supervision of hygiene, animal welfare, or meat safety inspection, (Report of the Expert Committee, 1987).

Out of the 3,600 licensed abattoirs in India, only two are mechanized and hygienic, and these are facing strong public opposition (India Today, January 11, 1996).

Article 51-A (g) of the Constitution of India states, "It shall be the fundamental duty of every citizen of India to protect and improve the natural environment... and to have compassion for all living creatures."

Euthanasia of suffering animals, according to the Prevention of Cruelty to Animals Act, is allowed if "it would be cruel to keep the animal alive" but only if the court, other suitable persons or police officers above the rank of the constable concur.

Because of the religious opposition to euthanasia, even of dying animals in severe pain, there is no legal requirement that the owner of such an animal should have it killed. Many orthodox Hindus and Jains oppose the killing of animals for any reason because they feel it is wrong to interfere in any way with another's karma or destiny.

Indians have reasoned that killing a sick cow is like killing your own mother and that is unthinkable.

But without more support from the central government and from foreign animal protection organizations, the plight of India's animals will worsen as the human population increases and resources become ever more scarce and costly.

* * * * *

Comments on Cow Protection

Cow protection is not a relic from the ancient past.

It's the heart of Dharma.

By supporting Gorakshana Seva programs, you are also protecting Mother Earth (symbolized by cow) through the promotion of environmentally sound farming practices. In one selfless stroke, you are sending valuable message to our children and to a troubled world which sees today's gentle cow as tomorrow's dinner.

It is the duty of every householder to have cows and bulls as household paraphernalia, not only for drinking milk but also for deriving religious principles." (Purport to Srimad Bhagavatam 1.17.2)

Most of us living in urban settings certainly cannot have cows and bulls as household paraphernalia". But as followers of the Vedas, as people upholding Dharma in the West, we can shelter the cows and bulls, and by so doing, teach the world about their value through your pious support.

We present here key scriptural verses from the Rig Veda and the cogent thoughts of Mahatma Gandhi on the subject of Goseva, caring for the cow, "the mother of Cosmic Forces."

Rig Veda: She is like the mother of the Cosmic Forces, the daughter of the cosmic Matter, the sister of cosmic Energy, the centre of the ambrosia. I address to men of wisdom-kill not her, the sinless inviolate cow.

The divine cow, herself is skilled in eloquence, gives speech to others, who comes surrounded by every kind of utterance, who helps me for my worship of the divine forces, it is only the fool that abandons her.

May cows come and bring us good fortune; let them stay in our cowsheds and be content in our company. May many colored cows bring here prolific milk for offerings to the resplendent Lord at many dawns!

The resplendent Lord bestows affluence on the devotee who offers worship and oblations. He takes not what belongs to the worshiper and gives him more; thereby increasing his wealth more and ever-more, he places the devotee in fortified positions, free from danger.

Let not the cows run away from us, let no thief carry them away; let no hostile weapon fall upon them. May the master of the cattle be long possessed of them, with the milk products of which he makes offerings and with which he serves the godly men.

Let not the cows fall a victim to the arrogant, evil foes. Let them not fall into the hands of a butcher or his shop. Let the cattle of the man, the householder, move about freely and graze without fear.

May the cows be our affluence; may the resplendent Lord grant us cattle; may the cows yield food (milk and butter) of the first libation. These cows, O men, are sacred as the Lord resplendent Himself-the Lord whose blessings we crave for, with head and heart.

O cows, you strengthen even the worn-out and fatigued and make the unlovely beautiful to look on. Your lowing is auspicious, and makes my dwelling prosperous. Great is the abundance that is attributed to you in our religious ceremony.

May you, O cows, have many calves grazing upon good pastures and drinking pure water at accessible ponds? May no thief be your master! May no best of prey assail you and may the dart of vital Lord never fall on you.

O resplendent Lord, a shower of virility as you are, may we have by your blessings the sturdy bulls for insemination and let us have plenty of nourishment for the cows.

Mahatma Gandhi: "The central fact of Hinduism is cow protection. Cow protection to me is one of the most wonderful phenomena in human evolution. It takes the human being beyond this species. The cow means the entire sub-human world. Man through the cow is enjoined to realize his identify with all that lives. Why the cow was selected for apotheosis is obvious to me.

The cows in India, the best companion!

She was the giver of plenty. Not only did she give milk, but she also made agriculture possible.

Cow protection is the gift of Hinduism to the world. And Hinduism will live so long as there are Hindus to protect the cow.

Hindus will be judged not by their tilaks, not by the correct chanting of mantras, not by their pilgrimages, not by their most punctilious observances of caste rules, but their ability to protect the cow.

I would not kill a human being to protect a cow, as I will not kill a cow to save a human life, be it ever so precious.

My religion teaches me that I should by personal conduct instill into the minds of those who might hold different views the conviction that cow-killing is a sin and that, therefore, it ought to be abandoned. My ambition is no less than to see the principle of cow protection established throughout the world.

But that requires that I should set my own house thoroughly in order first.

Cow protection to me is not mere protection of the cow. It means protection of all that lives and is helpless and weak in the world.

The cow is a poem of pity. One reads pity in the gentle animal. She is the mother to millions of Indian mankind. Protection of the cow means protection of the whole dumb creation of God. The ancient seer, whoever he was, began with the cow. The appeal of the lower order of creation is all the more forcible because it is speechless. The cow is the purest type of sub-human life. She pleads on behalf of the whole of the sub-human species for justice to it at the hands of man, the first among all that lives.

She seems to speak through her eyes "You are not appointed over us to kill us and eat our flesh or otherwise ill-treat us, but to be our friend and guardian. I worship it and I shall defend its worship against the whole world.

Mother Cow is in many ways equals the mother who gave us birth. Our mother gives us milk for couple of years and then expects us to serve her when we grow up. Mother Cow expects from us nothing but grass and grain".

The reader will observe that behind the foregoing requirements lies one thing, and that is ahimsa (non-injury), otherwise known as universal compassion. If that supreme thing is realized, everything else becomes easy. Where there is ahimsa, there is infinite patience, inner calm, discrimination, self-sacrifice and true knowledge.

Bhishma said:

No sacrifice can be performed without the aid of curds and ghee (clarified butter).

The very character of sacrifice which sacrifices have depends upon ghee. Hence ghee (or, the cow from which it is produced) is regarded as the very root of sacrifice.

Cows have been said to be the limbs of sacrifice. They represent sacrifice itself. Without them, there can be no sacrifice. With their milk and the Havi produced there from, they uphold all creatures by diverse acts. Cows are guileless in their behavior. From the flow sacrifices and havya and Kavya, and milk and curds and ghee. Hence cows are sacred.

Afflicted by hunger and thirst, they bear diverse burdens. Cows support the Munis (sages.)

Among all objects mobile and immobile, the mobile are superior. Among mobile creatures Brahmanas are superior.

The sacrifices are all established upon them. It is by sacrifice that Soma (nectar) is got. Sacrifice has been established upon cows. (For without ghee or clarified butter, which is produced from milk, there can be no sacrifice). The Gods become gratified through sacrifices. It is from the cows that the means have flowed of the sustenance of all the worlds. They yield Soma (nectar) in the form of milk. Cows are auspicious and sacred and grantor of every wish and givers of life!!

They who make gifts of cows, and who subsist upon the remnants of things offered as libations on the sacred fire, are regarded, as always performing sacrifices of every kind.

Of all kinds of gifts, the gift of cow is applauded as the highest. Cows are the foremost of all things. Themselves sacred, they are the best of cleansers and sanctifiers. People should cherish cows for obtaining prosperity and even peace. Cows are said to represent the highest energy both in this world and the world that is above. There is nothing that is more sacred or sanctifying than cows.

One should never feel any repugnance for the urine and the dung of the cow.

The Rishis (ascetic seers) discovered that the magnetism of the cows is something that is possessed of extraordinary virtues. Give the same kind of food to a cow and to a horse. The horse-dung emits an unhealthy stench, while the cow-dung is an efficacious disinfectant. There cannot be little doubt that the urine and dung of the cow possess untold virtues.

Vyasa Said:

Cows are sacred. They are embodiments of merit. They are high and most efficacious cleansers of all.

One should for three days drink the hot urine of the cow. For the next three days one should drink the hot milk of the cow. Having thus drunk for three days hot milk, one should next drink ghee for three days. Having in this way drunk hot ghee for three days, one should subsist for the next three days on air only.

Vasishtha Said:

By bathing in water mixed with cow-dung, people shall become sanctified. The deities and men shall use cow-dung for the purpose of purifying all creatures mobile and immobile. One can sit on dried cow dung. One should never eat the flesh of cows.

One should never show any disregard for cows in any way. If evil dreams are seen, men should take the names of cows. One should never obstruct cows in any way. Cows are the mothers of both the Past and the Future. Cows have become the refuge of the world. It is for this that cows are said to be highly blessed, sacred, and the foremost of all things. It is for this that cows are said to stay at the very head of all creatures. Every morning, people should bow with reverence unto cows.

Cows are the best Havi for the deities. The Mantras called Swaha and Vashat are forever established in cows. Sacrifices are established in the cows. Cows constitute the fruit of sacrifices. Cows are the future and the past, and Sacrifices rest on them. Morning and evening cows yield unto the Rishis, Havi for use in Homa (sacred fire ceremony).

Cows are always fragrant. The perfume emanated by the exudation of the Amytis Agallochum issues out of their bodies. Cows are the great refuge of all creatures. Cows constitute the great source of blessing unto all. (Swastayana is a ceremony of propitiation, productive of blessing and destructive of misery of every kind) Cows are the source of eternal growth.

Cows are sacred. They are the foremost of all things in the world. They are verily the refuge of the universe. They are the mothers of the very deities. They are verily incomparable.

Cows are the mothers of the universe. There is no gift more sacred than the gift to cows. There is no gift that produces more blessed merit.

Vyasa Said:

Cows constitute the stay of all creatures. Cows are the refuge of all creatures. Cows are the embodiment of merit. Cows are sacred and blessed and are sanctifiers of all.

One should never, in even one's heart, do an injury to cows. One should, indeed, always confer happiness on them.

Living in a pure state, in the midst of cows, one should mentally recite those sacred Mantras that are known by the name of Gomati, after touching pure water. By doing this, one becomes purified and cleansed. Brahmanas or righteous deeds, who have been cleansed by the knowledge, study of the Vedas, and observance of vows, should, only in the midst of sacred fires or cows or assemblies of Brahmanas, impart unto their disciples a knowledge of the Gomati Mantras which are every way like unto a sacrifice (for the merit they produce). One should observe a fast for three nights for receiving the boon constituted by knowledge of the import of the Gomati Mantras.

The man, who desirous of obtaining a son may obtain one by reciting these Mantras, He who desires the possession of wealth may have his desire gratified by adoring these Mantras.

The girl desirous of having a good husband may have her wish fulfilled by the same means. In fact, one may acquire the fruition of every wish one may cherish, by adoring these sacred Mantras.

When cows are gratified with the service one renders them, they are, without doubt, capable of granting the fruition of every wish. Even so, cows are highly blessed. They are the essential requisites of sacrifices. They are grantors of every wish. Know that there is nothing superior to cows.

Cows are endued with the elements of strength and energetic exertion. Cows have in them the elements of wisdom. They are the source of that immortality which sacrifice achieves.

They are the refuge of all energy. They are the steps by which earthly prosperity is won. They constitute the eternal course of the universe. They lead to the extension of one's race.

Bhishma Said:

One should not, by imparting knowledge of this ritual, benefit person that is not one's disciple or that is not observant of vows or that is bereft of faith or that is possessed of a crooked understanding. Verily, this religion is a mystery, unknown to most people. One that knows it should not speak of it at every place. There are, in the world, many men that are bereft of faith.

There are among men many persons that are mean and that resemble Rakshasas. This religion, if imparted unto them, would lead to evil.

It would be productive of equal evil if imparted to such sinful men as have taken shelter in atheism.

Together everyone should make an effort to promote the old custom of houses of cow protection, all householders, landlords, land owners, merchants, money-lenders etc should progress cow houses, from where can be gained ideal able-bodied cows and bulls. Nowadays the [lack] of establishment of grazing ground is lamentable. In this connection Manu wrote; - "On the four sides of every village and city there should be sufficient ground for pasture of cows." All capable farmers, landlords, merchants and money-lenders should make arrangement for centers to provide proper pasture for cattle. Also you should always consider advancing the cows.

The protection of the bovine species is prescribed by Hindu scripture. Orthodox Hindus are adamant that the nurture of cows lays at the core of Hindu Dharma, representing symbolically and in real, earthly terms the Hindu reverence for the Divine in all life. At a time when the human species is wrecking havoc on nature and the environment, cow protection takes on new meaning as a dramatic headline issue.

Schemes to slaughter and kill are the downfall of the cow and its progeny, and injure the holy and financial delights of both raja and subject. So for this reason everyone should make an effort to put a stop to these gristly practices. Several states have done laudable work in this connection, but unless central government will be compelled, it is impossible to satisfactorily inform of the effects. For the sake of this, effort should be made countrywide.

* * * * *

Usefulness and Utility Value of Cow Urine/Cow Dung

The cow gives milk and cream, yogurt and cheese, butter and ice cream, ghee and buttermilk. The milk of a cow is believed to promote Sattvic (purifying) qualities. The ghee (clarified butter) from the milk is used in ceremonies and in preparing religious food.

Cow dung is used as fertilizer, as a fuel and as a disinfectant in homes. Modern science acknowledges that the smoke from cow dung is a powerful disinfectant and an anti-pollutant. Its urine is also used for religious rituals as well as medicinal purposes. Cow as a symbol.

Omnipresent and omnipotent Almighty created millions and millions of creature in this vast universe. Amongst all the creatures, the cow is the most sacred, unique and magnificent creation.

Its usefulness is widespread. The cow dung is a fantastic antiseptic composition. Its milk offers iron, calcium and many valuable vitamins needed for human growth and its skin is utilized for bags and slippers for one and all.

Cow dung water sprinkled on the floor at the entrance prevents the spread of virus germs entering one's house. Mosquito coil producers use this cow dung to drive out mosquitoes. Biogas manufacturers hail the cow dung cakes as the most economical and unique fuel to produce power in the rural village.

While performing Homas, Yagnas and spiritual activities, the cow dung cakes are predominantly seen. Even when we breathe the last, it is the cow dung cakes, which cover our dead body, and in its flames our physical structure is burnt.

See how from birth to the end of our life the cow plays an important role with us. Its bones too act as a vital item for medicines. Along with the cows the OX too play an important role for feeding our stomach!

They plough the field to grow rice and other eatables daily seen in our kitchen. What a great creation it is?

Considerations of conscience aside, it was natural that in a predominantly agricultural and pastoral country like India, cows were and to some extent still are, considered to be the real wealth of the people.

After all it is the cow that gives birth to the bulls, bulls that are harnessed to plough the fields and to provide transportation. And then of course, there is the milk-milk that is cultured to become yoghurt-yoghurt which is churned to produce butter-butter which is converted into ghee or clarified butter that in India is used as cooking medium.

In addition to this, there is paneer or cottage cheese and buttermilk. Indians cannot forget khoya and manna-the other milk derivatives used in preparation of sweets. No wonder the cow is considered the backbone of rural society.

Paeans of praise are reserved for cow's milk and ghee which is considered to be an elixir. Dr. D. Bhandari, the former Director of Animal Husbandry in Rajasthan said, "You see it is the wonderful bacterial flora of the cow's stomach that imparts this matchless quality to its milk ideally balanced for humans.

Buffalo milk may be richer but it is the cow's milk that sharpens intellect, gives swiftness of body, stability of emotions and a serene nature to the one who drinks it."

Also taken, but in measured quantities, is cow urine or gau mutra which has a unique place in Ayurveda, the ancient Indian system of medicine. Commenting on the chemistry of Gau Mutra, Dr C.H.S. Sastry, Director of the National Institute of Ayurveda said, "Cow urine is used to produce a whole range of Ayurveda drugs, especially to treat skin diseases like eczema, besides gau mutra which is a well known disinfectant.

Anti-septic property is also the attribute of cow dung or gobar which is mixed with clay to form a plastering medium for mud huts. It is a proven fact that mud huts plastered with gobar keeps insects and reptiles away. This is the reason why people in the countryside still store grain in huge earthen pots plastered with gobar and gau mutra to keep it free from insect manifestations.

Gobar and gau mutras also mixed with mud and straw to make dried cakes that fuel kitchen fires. Traditional wisdom says that in burning these cow dung cakes, the temperature never rises beyond a certain point, ensuring the nutrients in the food are not destroyed by overheating.

Besides, the smoke of gobar clears the air of germs. Gobar has also been successfully used to produce bio-gas and generate electricity for consumer use. Scientific studies show that gobar has been found to be resistant to solar radiation. And of course, gobar mixed with gau mutra makes for excellent manure and a natural pesticide. Modern day ecologists are saying that as compared to chemical fertilizer which damages the land in the long run, gobar actually improves the health of the soil.

It isn't hard to see why Indian mythology says that Lakshmi, the goddess of wealth, resides in cow's gobar.

Usefulness of the cow forms the subject matter of an essay every child in India gets to write in primary school.

The children are told that even in dying, the cow gives us its hide which is prized for its softness. Besides the leather, the cow also gives its horns and bones and other parts of the body like intestines which have various uses.

However, there are other benefits of the cow which are beyond the survey of scientific scrutiny. Cow urine can cure cancer, impotence, sexually transmitted diseases, liver problems, tuberculosis, polio and obesity.

Eating red meat causes blindness, skin diseases and heart attacks.

It also results in divorce because eating red meat causes precocious sensuality in children, which later leads to impotence and ultimately divorce.

Out of cow urine/dung etc., by-products like Viboothi, Pesticide, Mosquito repellant, Bio-gas, Shampoo, Tooth powder, Medicinal preparations etc. will be scientifically manufactured and sold with the help of a leading bio technologist.

* * * * *

Cow - A Priceless Gift

Sages tell us, that no matter how advanced instrumentation may become, man will never be able to unravel the subtlety of the cow's qualities which are sung in the scriptures.

It isn't surprising that the cow is then actually worshipped. Big and small, there are many festivals all over India which are dedicated to the worship of the cow but none is as important as the Gopashtami celebrated with great fanfare especially in rural India. Besides the festivals there are also fairs all over the Indian country side where along with milk cows, colorful cow jewelry and clothing is also sold. I watched a farmer at Nagaur fair (in Rajasthan) buy a pair of silver horn jewelry for his cow with as much care and affection as was probably reserved for his wife!

But the romance of the cow is at dusk or what Indians call the hour of Gaudhuli-literally "cow dust". There is a mystique in the tinkling of cow bells as herds return from the days foraging, kicking up a clouds of dust just when the sun is going down. This is a special time, considered auspicious. So intimate is the cow's association with the lives of Hindus that in all the rites of passage of life, almost from conception to cremation, the cow is connected to ceremony and ritual.

Perhaps the most significant tribute to the cow is paid during Havana the formal fire ritual conducted by a priest. No Havana is said to be complete without the presence of Panchgavya or the five gifts of the cow, namely milk, yoghurt, ghee, gohar and gau mutra.

In the Hindu world view, to give cow charity or go daana is considered the highest and honorable act.

But if you cannot afford to give a cow in charity, you can certainly feed one. At an individual level, people routinely feed the cows-especially the wandering ones in the streets.

But what is unique to India are several institutions that look after the cow, chief among them is the Gaushala or "House of the Cow".

Conceptually different from the dairy, the gaushalas, the gau sadaus, the pinjara pols etc, maintain even the non-milking, old and sick cows along with those that are physically handicapped and need human care and attention for survival. As per the Office Secretary of the All India Gaushala Federation, there are more than 5000 Gaushalas in India which are charitable trusts managed by public funds.

There are many other institutions that also look after the interest of the cow. So, one really wonders how come cows are still on the streets? Talking to a wide cross section of people including bureaucrats, politicians, social workers, and those involved with the welfare of the cow, I found the answer as complex as the problem. In the final analysis, it is best to say that there is no will to act either by the people or by the State.

Maintaining status quo is the most expedient option. Summing up pithily, a government official said, "One should understand and accept the cows in the street as yet another paradox of contemporary India."

Perhaps this is the bane of modern times where ancient Indian values seem to be out of place in an industrial society. Traditionalist laments the apathy of educated urban Indians who are ambivalent in their feelings for the cow which seems to have become just another animal. They say that for a country known for its principles of vegetarianism and non-violence, it is a shame that not only is the cow treated so badly but also cow slaughter is still permitted in India.

Gandhi, the father of the nation made a passionate appeal to ban cow slaughter in India. He wrote with great depth of feeling for the cow and called it a "poem of compassion".

He said that the cow is the representative of the mute world of animals. With the language of its eyes the cow seems to be saying to Man that "God has not made you our master so that you could kill or eat or mistreat us. Instead he made you to be our friend and protector".

Such a fine thought can only emerge from this land where the cow is a symbol of its civilization. The song of glory of the cow is a priceless gift of India to the rest of the world.

The government of India decided to introduce a bill banning the sale of beef across India. Several reasons including a constitutional directive, economy and religious sentiments were cited as the reasons for the same.

Kerala and the north-eastern states have a large number of beef-eaters.

Should one eat an animal that a substantial chunk of the population consider as sacred?

Cow-A Jewel:

Sarvopanishado gaavo dogdha gopala nandhana: says the Gita. Krishna prefers to be called, Gopala and Govinda. The Yajur Veda begins with the invocation to the cows' Ishertovojetva.......... karmane - praying for their support in the conduct of Yagnas. Again Krishna declares in the Gita (10.28) Dhenunamasmi kaamadhuk- among the cows I am Surabhi and Kamadhenu. In the Puranas we have the reference to Kamadhenu springing from Samudra Mathana, as one of the jewels of the ocean along with Lakshmi.

The general prayer after the holy rituals just as yagnas, homas is for the grant of protection to the Cows and Brahmins. Go brahmanebhyo shubhamastu nityam loka: samastha: sukhino bhavanthu, which ensures the well being of all the worlds.

In the common parlance we have the adage Janani janma bhoomi: go matha cha swargaadapi gareeyasi-one's own mother, the motherland and the mother cow are greater in value than the heavens. Shri Andal the lady saint of Sri Vaishnavite culture in her 'Thiruppavai' describes the cows as 'Vallal Perum Pashukkal'- meaning thereby that they suckle not only their calves but also all of us, treating us as her own children. To quote the Vedas again, "All protection bestow on us Lord Narayana, Vishnu! Please protect our cows which give all the necessary ingredients for performing a Yagna the cow".

All the 33 million Gods reside in her. The Paramathma, the Absolute Brahman takes His adobe in the sacred heart of the cow. According to 'Go Smriti' wherever cows reside Lord Vishnu lives in those places. The Asura Hiranya Kashipu knew that truth and as a Vishnudrohi he asked his men to destroy the places sheltering cows.

In India they make an Elixir, for purification known as Panch Gavyam out of five ingredients pertaining to the cow (its milk, curd, ghee, dung and urine) for Paapa Nashanam and Dosha Nirmoolanam. All the sins and defects referred to as the Taapatrayaas, the Aadyaatmika, the Adhibouthika and Aadhidaivika aspects of our lives are removed by the Pancha Gavya Praasanam.

Cattle Welfare Concerns

Because of a seasonal and regional lack of fodder (and water), and because of overstocking and overgrazing, many cattle suffer from chronic malnutrition.

This in turn weakens their immune systems and makes them susceptible to parasitic infestations and other diseases. Large numbers of poorly nourished cattle create a potent medium for outbreaks of infectious diseases which necessitate costly vaccinations, which are too often ineffectual due to inadequate refrigeration.

There is also the widespread belief that there is not real cattle surplus, and that India would do better with even more cattle because their organic manure is so valuable to agriculture.

The environmental damage in some regions from overgrazing is especially caused by "scrub" cattle that are kept simply as manure makers before they are driven to slaughter or die. Their sad existence in semi-starvation, often also chronically sick, will continue without mass public education and government assistance.

Cattle Shelters

The first animal shelters in India began with the advent of Buddhism, to whom King Asoka (269-232 BC) converted. Asoka ruled over much of the Indian subcontinent, converting millions to accept Buddhism, and was the first to set up shelters and animal hospitals, although some historians believe that Buddha himself was the first to do so. Asoka put compassion into action, by caring for animals in need, and into the law also, setting up wildlife preserves and punishments for those who abused and killed animals.

Goshala and pinjrapoles are located throughout India and are supported by taxes and charitable donations from the business community. Goshala are refuges for cattle, often linked with the Hindu cult of Krishna, while pinjrapoles serve as a refuge for a more diverse animal population, including birds, other wild animals, and even insects and microorganisms in collected piles of household dust.

A government census found there were 3,000 animal shelters maintaining some 6, 00,000 cattle and thousands of other animals from deer to dogs and camels to cats.

Even though Indians know that the buffalo is a better quality milk producer than most varieties of cows, buffaloes are rarely found in Goshalas because they are considered unclean and not worthy of the same respect as cows.

The Goshala Development Scheme implemented in the 1957-1961 five-year plan to provide subsidies to improve exiting Goshalas were more successful during some periods than others since their implementation.

We should see that Goshalas that keep dry and cattle that cannot be rehabilitated for draught work operate at a deficit. Attempts to make them more productive are not likely to significantly reduce this deficit and so without adequate community and government funding, as is the case in many places in India, cattle will suffer a fate surely worse than the butcher's knife.

This should not take place and all should join hands to support this Goshala movement. All should shoulder the Goshalas activities with funds, physical involvement and full of devotion.

There were some cruel incidents to be looked into. For example according to the Indian Express (Coimbatore, February 25, 1997), the local authorities tied up a huge wild bull on the rampage. It was decided to auction off the creature for slaughter, which fetched much opposition from the devout. Someone killed the bull with some poison during the night to "save it from being defiled by the butcher's knife".

Cattle Death Drivers

Millions of old, spent cows, exhausted bullocks, and young male calves are driven on foot up to 300 miles, or are crammed into trucks for transit into Kerala, or in railroad cars to West Bengal, the two states where cattle slaughter is legal. Their often bleeding, worn down hooves make hardly any sound as they pass by. Veterinarian Dr. Ghanshyam Sharma from Sikkim, in the Northeast of India where Cow slaughter is also legal, sees cattle coming in from Jammu, Kashmir, Bihar, and Nepal.

He observes, "Often entire hooves of these animals are snuffed out and gunny bags are tied around the wounded stumps and this way they walk. "Many sustain injuries being loaded and off-loaded during part of the journey or die in transit.

Some collapse on the way, are beaten, and even have salt and hot chilies rubbed into their eyes and have their tails hammered, twisted, and broken to make them get up and keep walking. Some of those being transported get trampled and suffocate, or have an eye gouged out by another's horn. Water and fodder are rarely provided during their long journeys, and even at rest stops.

As per a report, one million cows are taken every year to slaughter houses in Kerala from other southern states, for slaughtering" (**India Today,** January 11, 1996.)

Journalist Subhashini Raghavan, in her exposure of these cattle death marches, found a complex network of middlemen traders, "who are calloused by constant exposure to cruelty" and they develop the attitude that" if an animal is slotted for slaughter, it ceases to be a living being with pain, hunger and terror."

Raghavan found that vast numbers of cattle are made to walk hundreds of miles through pedestrian side-roads to escape checkpoints, en route to regional markets from local markets and then on to transfer points where they may then be put into trucks.

He concludes his articles stating that, "throughout the length and breadth of this birthplace of Ahimsa, the tragic march of the condemned continues unabated-a poignant symbol of our callousness, in even denying the last comforts and dignity of those who lived their lives serving us." (**The Hindu**, April 16, 1995)

*****

Political view point

Cow protection became a political icon for Hindus.

Their ritual slaughter of buffalo, sheep and goats is looked down on by Hindus. Pre-slaughter stunning eliminates the need to cast the animal onto the ground prior to having its throat cut, thus eliminating much fear associated with being cast.

For Mohandas Gandhi, cow protection was an important aspect of Indian independence from British colonial rule, figuring in the return to traditional values.

"Although Buddhism was a major vehicle for the spread of the ahimsa concept throughout India and indeed throughout much of Asia, never carried the doctrine to the extremes of Jainism. In Buddhist thinking, ahimsa became a positive adjunct to moral conduct stemming from the cardinal virtue of compassion rather than the all-encompassing negative principle of non-activity of the 'Jains".

* * * * *

Agricultural Modernization, Politics and Cattle Welfare

Many native peoples have been made landless by agricultural "modernization" and migrate in increasing numbers to the cities along with their few animals and possessions. The high cattle population in the nation's capital Delhi is evidence enough. In 1995 some 50 cattle per day were killed or severely injured by traffic reports a Newsletter.

The Prevention of Cow Slaughter Act of 1955, which allows the slaughter of cattle that are diseased, disabled, or more than 15 years old, allegedly resulted in young, nonproductive cows having their legs hacked and broken so they could be legally slaughtered. The Bharatiya Janata Party (BJP) banned all slaughter of the bovine species when it gained control of Delhi in 1994, purportedly to tighten various laxities in the prohibition of cow slaughter.

The BJP voiced Mohandas Gandhi who told all India in 1921 that, "Hindus will be judged... by their ability to protect the cow."

During the tumultuous 1996 elections, the Vishnu Hindu Parishad (VHP) party, "ignoring the facts and problems" of cattle overpopulation, starvation, disease and suffering, according to India Today (January 11, 1996), launched an anti-cattle slaughter campaign.

A saint said "The trembling and wailing of the cows being slaughtered lead to earthquakes".

According to a 1992 Indian Market Research Bureau survey reported in this article, 74.2% of urban households are non-vegetarian, the majority consuming mutton, fish, and chicken, and some 12.7% beef. (How much is buffalo meat is not clear)

When the BJP won control of the central government in May 1996, the new President Sri Shankar Dayal Sharma announced in his opening of Parliament address a total ban nationwide on cow slaughter as one of the new government's policy agendas.

The toxic chemicals that most of India's tanneries continue to discharge into rivers and watersheds cause serious ecological and human health problems. While some 200 million people are malnourished in India, the country exported US$625 million worth of wheat and flour, and US$1.3 billion of rice in 1995.

A copy of the letter dated June 20, 1994, from the Secretary of the Akhil Bharat Krishi-Goseva Sangh Society of Bombay, which claims to be engaged in the preservation and protection of the "cattle wealth" of India, states:

"Our efforts towards preservation of cattle wealth at the political level are not meeting with the desired success in our country in view of the thick skinned bureaucracy and politicians who are hell bent on destroying the cattle wealth of our nation at the behest of the meat lobby, which finds enormous wealth in this activity as also at the behest of FAP, an organ of United Nations which dictates policies in third world countries, aiming at total destruction of the cattle resources of third world countries.

"However there is a silver lining to this otherwise discouraging scenario and those silver linings is in the form of our judiciary. Some time back a case instituted in a court in New Delhi involving shifting of a slaughterhouse from one area of Delhi City to another area, the Learned Judge who delivered a judgment in this case has made an excellent analysis of the whole issue and established the legal rights of animals as well as the need for conserving animals for conservation of environment. He has established that the human race, the environment and the animals are interrelated and extinction of animals will spell doom for environment and mankind."

What is called for is a unified sensibility that integrates the symbolic, material economic, emotional, social and spiritual components of the human-cow/cattle relationship into a mutually enhancing symbiosis.

The human side of the relationship is more balanced and equitable when the rights, interests, and welfare of animals are given equal and fair consideration.

The ethical inconsistencies in the religious and secular communities attitude toward and treatment of cattle and other animals is more evident in India than in other countries precisely because India is the birthplace of the highest spiritual principles pertaining to animal welfare and yet they are not always put into practice, creating an essentially schizoid situation between the ideal and the real.

Caring for animals and caring for people, for the poor and the hungry, go hand in hand as part of the humane agenda of any democratic society. While we focus particularly on India's cattle, the plight of these creatures mirrors the plight of the poor. There are no miracle remedies for hunger and poverty from advances in technology, science, or medicine.

The miracle will come not via genetic engineering of animals and plants but through the transformation of humanity into a compassionate, empathic, and responsible life form. A mutually enhancing symbiosis with the Earth community of plants and animals, both wild and domesticated, is our only viable future.

Our hope lies in our capacity to reconnect empathically with all living beings and to use sound science and policies as our instruments, and compassion as our compass.

* * * * *

Neelavara Goshala Kshetra

Where is this Neelavara?

In India, the Dhakshana Karnataka is the southern part of Karnataka state.

In this State we have Udupi 60kms from Mangalore.

To reach Mangalore we have trains like Mangalore Mail, Mangalore Express, West Coast Express, Rapti Sagar Express, Lakshadweep Mangalore Express, Rajdhani Express, Navyug Express, etc. An airport also operates to enable faster reach to Mangalore. Indian Airlines and Jet Airways operate their services to carry passengers from all over India to Mangalore.

Udupi is a beautiful pilgrim centre where one can visit Lord Sri Krishna temple in which the main deity was installed by Shri Madhwacharya, the great Madhva saint who is no one else but incarnation of Sri Vayu & Bheema. From this holy place by road, we can reach Neelavaram (which is only 18 Km from Udupi)

A beautiful green surroundings and pleasant breeze will welcome one and all to the Neelavara Goshala formed by Paramapoojya Sri Vishwaprasanna Theertha Swamiji. It is a rejoicing site to see all the cows moving about merrily as they have escaped from the evil hands of the unkind inhuman slaughter-houses.

As they are fed and well attended and well monitored, they rejoice every second in that heavenly place. They are very very fortunate to be fed by the revered Swamiji with his own friendly hands. With His personal visit, every cow enjoys a holy association. His Holiness curdles them, pats them and greets them with smile and favor which enables them to gain strength, joy and vigor which they had lost due to negligence in the hands some unworthy ruthless men.

What a gracious welfare! What a heavenly atmosphere! Their health is taken care with appropriate medicine and timely attention. Once the Swamiji enter the premises all the cows sound 'mmAAA' and greets him with warmth. They thank him for his good deeds and grace with which they have been lifted to lofty heights of peace and happiness. Two large wells have been dug for growing rich green trees around them. What an environ-friendly atmosphere! What a nice green peaceful arena, which makes the cows breathe fresh air free from city, pollution and dirt.

Neelavara Goshala is absolutely a Brindavan for these neglected, ignored and thrown away cows without mercy. This is a beginning of a new life for them with enriching spirit, freshness and faith.

More than 1200 cows are seen and everyday cows from various States are brought whenever any danger, ill-treatment, sickness and uncared situation attack them. Each and every cow thanks wholeheartedly the Swamiji's praiseworthy actions which have created a revolution in the history of Hindu faith and cows at large. Visitors for this green cow shelter are from various States.

Pejawar mutt junior pontiff Shri Vishwaprasanna Theertha Swamiji, with motherly care looks after all the visitors and his kindness pleases their heart immensely. His vision for cow's well-being is immaculate with the divine blessing of Lord Sri Krishna whom He worships.

Many VIPs, Donors, philanthropists have visited this unique green surrounding and passed words of praise. They have exhilarated and rejoiced after seeing the arrangements. The donors have been benefited with 80G tax concessions.

* * * * *

Honorable Services of Shri Pejawar Mutt Swamijis

Kodavur a small hamlet near Udupi, Karnataka, is providing shelter for aged cows for the past 17 years on a land spread over 2 acres. As the number of cows brought to this goshala increased the Neelavara Goshala was started. Revered Shri Shri Pejawar Matha Junior Swamiji Poojyashree Shri Shri Vishwaprasanna Theertha Swamiji has taken invaluable efforts to set up Goshala at Neelavara near Udupi, on an area of 25 acres, a unique place for neglected cows and cows in pitiable status.

If any cow is known to be taken for slaughtering for obtaining skin, flesh for earning income, then His Holiness immediately rushes and see that cows are rescued and taken to Neelavaram for shelter and safe custody. "Whatever income you expect to get from slaughtering, I will pay you and take these cows to my Neelavaram for complete well being with food, medicine, shelter and with all personal protection with dedication & love" says His holiness with mercy and care for the sacred cows.

Such is the miraculous work done by His Holiness under the name 'Govardhanagiri Trust'. If any cow is seen lying on the street or anywhere with ill health of injury after an accident or uncared, then immediately the revered Shri Vishwaprasanna Theertha Swamiji sees that those cows are escorted and transported to this health care taking arena.

With day & night service men are posted to help these neglected sacred creations. Some may let off cows, which are unable to give milk or sometimes try to convert it to beef for feeding some inhuman beings. Then at these instances Neelavara project men see that they are prevented from getting slaughtered or ignored in inhuman way.

The Senior Swamiji Poojyashree Sri Vishvesha Theertha Swamiji has walked miles together in Haryana State, braving mud, stone, storm, hot sun, rain, slush and bush to fight for these pitiable cows from being butchered. His noble dedication for the welfare has won admiration from all VIPs and dignitaries all over the world. His unique and yeomen services have saved many hundred cows, which were in pathetic condition. Even now cows from Delhi, Haryana, Punjab, Gujarat and many north Indian states come here to Neelavara for shelter and peaceful life.

They are really fortunate to spend their final part of their life in this peace loving arena. When transported from other states the Revered Swamijis are strict in seeing that they are transported in such a way that not more than 5 are in one lorry and that too with sufficient water, grass and food items for the cows to travel comfortably. Usually these cows are dumped mercilessly with no place to move their tails too or no space to breathe. Such atrocities are totally curbed by the Revered Swamijis. Their holy efforts are adored by one and all over the world.

* * * * *

Profile of Paramapujya Shri Vishwesha Tirtha Swamiji

Major Milestones

27-4-1931 Born at Ramakunjja (Village near to Kukke Subrahmanya)

3-12-1938 Sanyasa Diksha Sweekara and renamed as Shri Vishvesha Thirtha Swamiji

1943-Presidentship in Shri Madhwaraddantha Samvardhaka Sabha

1952 to 1954-1st 'Paryaya' and Pooja to Udupi Shri Krishna

4-1-1953-Establishing 'Akhila Bharata Madhwa Mahamandala'

28-7-1956-Establishing 'Poorna Prajna Vidyapeetha' at Bangalore

1959-'Bhashya Mangala' at Badarinath

1968to1970-2nd 'Paryaya' and Pooja to Udupi Shri Krishna

1968-Publishing the book "Gitasaroddhara'

1968-Inauguration of Shri Krishna Chikitsalaya at Udupi

1970-1980-Publication of Sarvamoola Granthas

1978-Inauguration of 'Udupi Chatra' at Badarinath

1983-Shri Krishna Pratishta at Poorna Prajna Vidyapeetha

1984to1986-3rd 'Paryaya' and Pooja to Udupi Shri Krishna

1985 Shri Krishna Pratistha Saptashatamanotsava

1988-Golden Jubilee celebration of Peetharohana

1989-Bhakthi Ratha Yatra with Madhwa Statue and Pratistapana at Badarinath

1991-Shastyabdi Poorti at Tirumala

1992-Chaturmasya at Badarinath

1998-Sudhamangala at Pajaka Kshetra

2000-Sudhamangala at Pajaka Kshetra

2000 to 2002-4th 'Paryaya' and Pooja to Udupi Shri Krishna

2005-25th Sudhamangala & Golden Jubilee Celebration of Poorna Prajna Vidyapeetha at Bangalore.

2008 26th Sudhamangala at Mysore. Later conducted Sudha Mangala in various Divine locations and pilgrim centers and finally in 2019 completed 38 Sudha Mangalas.

2016-2018 Historic 5th Udupi Paryaya

Established Sujnana Satram (A Branch of Vishwesha Sevaka Sangha)

For enquiry into puranas, conducting monthly discourses by various Vidwan on Ramayana, Mahabharatha, Srimad Bhagavatham, Bhagawat Gita, Puranas etc.,

Releasing CDs as Jnana Karya are some of the salient activities.

Holy Brindavana - 29th Dec 2019

* * * * *

Profile of Paramapoojya Shri Vishwaprasanna Thirtha Swamiji

(Junior Pontiff of Shri Pejavar Matha, Udupi. (Born 1964))
Vidya Guru: Shri Vidyamanya Thirtha Swamiji &
Shri Vishwesha Tirtha's Swamiji
Institutions Attended
Vedanta Studies at Admaru Gurukula, Udupi
Sanskrit College, Udupi
Sudhadhyayana at Shri Vishwesha Thirtha Swamiji
1988-Sanyasa Sweekara & Pranavopadesha by Shri Vishwesha Thirtha Swamiji
1991-Sudhamangala at Tirumala
Publishing the Kannada Magazine-"Achara-Vichara"
Various Activities
Under guidance of Shri Vishwesha Thirtha Swamiji
1999-Established Prahlada Gurukula at Udupi
2003-Published the English Magazine-"Achara-Vichara"
Renovation work at Muchhilakodi Shri Subrahmanya Temple
2004-Established Govardhanagiri Goshala at Neelavara.
Up to 2019 successfully conducted more than 30 Padayatras.

Undertaking Dikvijaya Sanchara entire length and breadth of the country, Blessing the Devotees with Bhiksha/Pada Pooja/Upadesha/Devotional Pravachana

Establishment of Vishwa Janeena Trust Sumedha School for mentally challenged children at Neelavara.

2013- Erection of Sri Kaliya Mardhana temple surrounded by a huge water tank containing water from all sacred rivers in India. Pithru sala, guest house, dining hall, kitchen for conducting all rituals in Neelavara goshala were also established by his Holiness.

* * * * *

Pithru Tharpana

It's a part of Pithru Yagna on holy days for the grant of wealth, long life for us and for our children involves a serious rite of devotion using sesame seeds, water and the prescribed text to be recited by a Vedic priest. If one could not get the entire above, one need not lose heart but take faith and confidence and do Go Pradakshana - going round the cow and submitting our helplessness with joined hands in appeal to its mercy.

The great poet Kalidasa narrates beautifully the heart moving story in his epic 'Raghuvamsa'. King Dileepa and Queen Sudakshinaa had no children and as per the advice of sage Vashishta performed austere service to the celestial cow Nandini the child of Kamadhenu for 21 long days. As a result of this cow worship the Queen gave birth to a son who was to become the great King Raghu.

All of us know the great story how King Viswaraata became Brahmarishi Vishwaamitra over his capture of Nandini in the ashram of Vashishta. The Chyavana Maharshi episode in the Shanthi Parva (51/22) of the Maha Bharatha is a telling example of the greatness of the cow. The Maharishi was performing severe austerities for twelve years in water and in Samadhi. Accidentally he was caught in a fisherman's net. They begged his forgiveness but the Rishi saw the death caused to the fishes and he also wanted to embrace death.

The fisherman ran to King Nahusha and asked him to intervene. The sage asked the King to remedy the loss suffered by them. The King ordered the grant of a thousand old coins equivalent to the sage. When a doubt arose to the exact value assessment, the King raised it to one hundred thousand gold coins.

The sage asked the King to get his ministers' counsel for its verification; the King further raised the grant to ten million gold coins. The Sage did not give his assent. The King was prepared to gift half of his kingdom as the deeming value. When he did not get the sage's nod, he was ready to forgo his entire kingdom. The Sage was not happy.

The King became sad and consulted another sage who was observing intense austerities. That Maharishi said that a Brahma Gnani's worth cannot be estimated. He opined that in the same fashion the value of a cow cannot be ascertained. Because Brahmanas are the embodiments of mantras and the cows are the embodiments of divine havis-food. He advised him to give a cow as an equivalent to the value of a sage.

Chyavana Maharishi accepted the assessment and praised the greatness of the cows. He told the King that hearing about the praise of the cows and donation of cows, looking after the cows and even the Dharshan of cows are considered good deeds according to Shastras.

Cows are Punya personified. They shower prosperity like Goddess Lakshmi. A good shepherd can himself, like Gopala, absolve people of their sins. Cows are the main gates to heaven. They give Havis to the Gods. Even Aadishesha with one thousand heads cannot describe its true worth. The King donated cows to the fisherman and the fishermen along with fishes went up to heaven. The Sage blessed the King for his faith and devotion to the cause of worship of the cow.

Tasmat Sarva Prayathnena Go aradhanam Kuru. Samrakshanam Kuru.

Hence worship and take care of the cows with all your efforts.

* * * * *

Godhana

The Special greatness of the treasure of cows is pointed out in the Dharma Shastra:

"Sarveshhaameva BhuutaanaaM gaavaH sharaNamutamam." Thus all proclaim that the cow being enjoyed by everyone is to be protected.

Hindu culture is filled to the brim with this sentiment:-

"Yad hgR ihe duHkhitaa gaavaH sa yaati narake naraH."

The man who gives suffering to the cow goes to hell.

But our civilization and culture have become intermixed with the culture of Westerners, from that time, the extensive disappearance of the Indian method of teaching has caused ignorance of the Shastra, Purana etc-that the cow, the Brahmana etc are the same, this devout scriptural knowledge is disappearing.

Today it is usual to be pleased at measuring the material weight of the cow stock; but remember now of the subtler-than-the subtlest of material knowledge of cow stock, of the excellent dharma and usefulness, the very whereabouts may not [now] be connected with, that was evident through supernatural powers to that Indian law-giver.

The greatness and holiness of cow stock, in you is one which is subtler-than-the-subtlest, the cause and form, the reason of keenness of the elements, for their investigation and knowledge the yantra (instrument) of modern material scientists will always remain too crude. Right here is also the cause of the clever twentieth century knowledge remaining unsuccessful in the understanding of the real truth the secret that in the hairs on the body of the mother cow the gods are dwelling, and the dawn sighting of a cow, the worship of the cow, the cow-god etc.

The universal feeling is held of the holiness of the cow herds and that one bears the truth to oneself by way of intellect, attainable experience, or confident in the way of the Shastra, not by physical instruments.

According to Skanda Purana every part of the cow houses a deity. Brahma is in her back, Vishnu in her throat, Rudra (i.e. Shiva) is established on her face, and Moon are in her eyes, Yama and Indra on the tips of the horns, the Ashvins in her nostrils, Lakshmi and Ganga behind her tail, etc.

Dharmashastra then is indeed a description of the greatness and sanctity of Godhana (cow wealth), but in the Indian Arthashastra is the special importance of Gopalan (cow protection). In the Arthashastra (science of wealth) of kautilya we meet with a comprehensive explanation of cow custody and cow protection.

The Arthashastra commands that earth that is not being cultivated is made into grazing ground for cattle. This manner of property of cattle strongly cherished both wealth and dharma. From wealth indeed desires are fulfilled and from dharma is moksha (salvation). Thence from Godhana (cow wealth) wealth, dharma, desire and moksha-the four are gained.

Therefore in Indian life property in cattle is highly valued. Who puts faith in the Hindu Dharmashastra ought to have the reward of wealth and success for service to the cow and progressing the cow herd according to the regulations of Shastra, and those who do not put their faith in the Dharmashastra, they want wealth and fulfillment of desires and will make an effort to progress the cow stock and protect cows according to the regulation of Arthashastra.

For those who believe only in tangible proof, [think of] the abundant kindness of the mother cow, what might be the pleasure of eating grass the whole life and donating milk and ghee which contains nutritive matter.

If they have been grateful to Gomatha (mother cow), then, afterwards, might they not weigh up a small portion of humaneness. In brief it can be said that the mother cow is an advantage to the society of man, from this the human race is always indebted to the mother cow.

* * * * *

Lord Krishna and the Cows

Lord Krishna adored the cows and said in Gita that he loved them and consider it nearest to his holy heart. He is also named as Gokula Krishna too for the admiration and love showed towards them. You can see Lord Krishna in any painting, sculpture or an art work accompanied by sacred cows. When He played melody on the flute, the happy cows surrounded Him and ran with joy wherever he went. His association made the cows holy and great. It had stolen His grace and passion. When there was a heavy flood & rain & thunder, Lord Krishna came to the rescue by lifting Govardhanagiri (Mountain) and created a shelter to all the cows.

Why not we also raise a finger of protest, with all firm, faith & vigor to prevent the cow's slaughters and merciless treatments?

To propagate cow's protection, essay competitions, oratorical competitions can be held in all school & colleges to emphatically sow in them the seeds of mercy and love for this nice creation on this mother earth. Cows are said to be our mother and worshipful women on earth. If that is done why not many journals meant for women release special numbers, supplements highlighting the mercy to be shown to this second mother for all of us.

When it was asked "What will happen in Kali Yuga?" immediately the scene shown to him was beating and torturing of a cow.

This will be the status of Kaliyuga say the puranas and Vedas. So when we are passing the Kaliyuga phase, we have to stoutly protest it and take measures to safeguard cows from ill treatments & tortures.

That cautious announcement by the Vedas only alerts us and tells us "beware of this ill treatment". Take steps to crush it. Make sure that you protect those cows or they will perish. Make rules and amend it to see that they are safe-guarded. Why not we prove that we are aware of this danger to our sacred cows and we cannot be silent spectators for their cruel treatment.

In every email you send it to your friends see that a verse on cow protection and cow greetings is sent to enlighten them and be a part and parcel of this great movement. Educate the youth as they are the greatest source of energy and vigor for all good things to happen. Once they are awakened then the entire nation will awake and come forward to shoulder the pain of our motherly cows.

No time to waste! No time to be silent. Awake!

* * * * *

Conclusion

Man has evolved from lower form of life. We are, therefore, related to the whole creation. The principle of cow protection symbolizes human responsibility to the subhuman world. It also indicates reverence for all forms of life. The cow serves humans throughout its life, and even after death. The milk of the cow runs in our' blood. Its contributions to the welfare of the family and the community are countless. Hindus pray daily for the welfare of cows. When the cows are cared for, the world at all levels will find happiness and peace.

The cow is Aghanya-that which may not be slaughtered

The cow represents the entire animal kingdom and is man's link to the dumb animals of creation. In respecting the cow, we are showing respect for all living things, a notion that ties in deftly with ahimsa and vegetarianism. This point of view was propagated by Gandhi.

To the Hindu, the cow symbolizes all others creatures. The cow is a symbol of the Earth, the nourisher, the ever-giving, undemanding provider. The cow represents life and the sustenance of life. The cow is so generous, taking nothing but want grass and grain. It gives and gives and gives of its milk, as does the liberated soul give of his spiritual knowledge. The cow is so vital to life, the virtual sustained life, for many humans. The cow is a symbol of grace and abundance. Veneration of the cow instills in Hindus the virtues of gentleness, receptivity and connectedness with nature.

The only cow-question for Hindus is, "Why don't more people respect and protect this remarkable creature?"

In the Hindu tradition, the cow is honored, garlanded and given special feedings at festivals all over India, most importantly the annual Gopashtama festival. Demonstrating how dearly Hindus love their cows, colorful cow jewelry and clothing is sold at fairs all over the Indian countryside. From a young age, Hindu children are taught to decorate the cow with garlands, paint and ornaments. Her nature is epitomized in Kamadhenu, the divine, wish-fulfilling cow.

The cow and her sacred gifts like milk and ghee in particular are essential elements in Hindu worship, penance and rites of passage. In India, more than 5,000 institutions called Gaushalas, maintained by charitable trust, care for old and infirm cows. And while many Hindus are not vegetarians, most respect the still widely held code of abstaining from eating beef. By her docile, tolerant nature, the cow exemplifies the cardinal virtue of Hinduism, non-injury, known as ahimsa. The cow also symbolizes dignity, strength, endurance, maternity and selfless service. In the Vedas, cows represent wealth and joyous Earthly life.

From the Rig Veda (4.28.1; 6) we read. The cows have come and have brought us good fortune. In our stalls, contented, may they stay! May they bring forth calves for us, many-colored, giving milk for Indra each day? You make, O cows, the thin man sleek; to the unlovely you bring beauty. Rejoice our homestead with pleasant lowing. In our assemblies we laud your vigor."

Let us not be silent spectator of all evil happenings to our beloved sacred Mother – the Cow.

Let us all join together to protect them and extend all support to GOSHALAS where they are adorned and taken care of.

One such Goshala is at Neelavara and let us all utilize this opportunity give a big hand to serve monetarily and physically.

During the Rathotchava (car festival) we can see many people joining together to pull the chariot. So also for this great movement to protect the cows, everybody's efforts are needed. Let us all pull the chariot of success in this venture.

The great Swamijis of Pejawar mutt have shown the way for cow protection thro' goshala at Neelavara, which we shall follow with devotion and care and attain eternal bliss.